Merry Christmas!

D Reid

You Know It's CHRISTMAS When . . .

You Know It's CHRISTMAS When . . .

THE STATLER BROTHERS'

DON REID

with

DEBO REID and LANGDON REID

PREMIUM PRESS AMERICA
NASHVILLE, TENNESSEE

You Know It's Christmas When . . . by Don Reid with Debo Reid and Langdon Reid

Published by PREMIUM PRESS AMERICA

ISBN 1-887654-51-8
Library of Congress Catalog Number 2005909111

PREMIUM PRESS AMERICA gift books are available at special discounts for premiums, sales promotions, fund-raising, or educational use. For details contact the Publisher at P.O. Box 159015, Nashville, TN 37215, or phone toll free (800) 891-7323 or (615) 256-8484, or fax (615) 256-8624.

www.premiumpressamerica.com

Design by Armour&Armour, Nashville, Tennessee
www.armour-armour.com

First Edition October 2006
1 2 3 4 5 6 7 8 9 10

To
Caroline and Sela
and everyone
who loves Christmas

You know it's Christmas when . . .

You go to the Christmas parade and hear a sweetly, out-of-tune band play "Winter Wonderland."

You watch *Miracle on 34th Street* . . . in black and white . . . the one with John Payne and Maureen O'Hara.

You've slept through a Christmas cantata.

You know it's Christmas when . . .

You and your dog fall asleep on
the floor by the tree after supper.

You've made batches of chocolate peanut butter balls, coconut macaroons, and sugar cookies cut into the shape of Christmas trees.

You've *eaten* batches of chocolate peanut butter balls, coconut macaroons, and sugar cookies cut into the shape of Christmas trees.

You go to a church pageant and see little kids playing Mary and Joseph and a doll baby playing Jesus.

You've slept on flannel reindeer sheets.

One strand of lights goes out on the tree.

You know it's Christmas when . . .

Your kids have written
their letters to Santa Claus.

They hear Santa read their letters
on the radio or TV or see
them printed in the newspaper.

Someone says they heard
it was calling for snow
on Christmas Eve.

You know it's Christmas when . . .

You see that commercial on TV
with the horse and the sleigh
with "I'll Be Home For Christmas"
playing in the background.

All the kids are home from college.

You reminisce to yourself
about each ornament as you
put it on the tree.

The Night Before Christmas Quiz

According to the poem "The Night Before Christmas:"

1. Who wrote it?
2. What visions danced in the children's heads and what are they?
3. What line is not in the poem:
   - A. The crest of the moon through the falling of snow
   - B. As dry leaves that before the wild hurricane fly
   - C. More rapid than eagles his coursers they came
4. How big was:
   - A. Santa
   - B. His sleigh
   - C. The reindeer
5. How many reindeer?
6. Name them.
7. Which reindeer in some printings has another name and what is it?
8. How was Santa dressed?
9. What color were his boots?
10. What does Santa say as he drives out of sight?

Bonus: What is the correct title of this poem?

Answers

1. Clement C. Moore
2. Sugarplums—a sugar-coated candy
3. A. The crest of the moon through the falling of snow
4. A. Elf

   B. Miniature

   C. Tiny
5. Eight
6. Dasher, Dancer, Prancer, Vixen, Comet, Cupid, Donner, Blitzen
7. Donner is often Donder
8. “He was dressed all in fur from his head to his foot”
9. No boots are mentioned—no red suit either
10. “Happy Christmas to all, and to all, a good night”

Bonus: “A Visit From St. Nicholas”

You know it's Christmas when . . .

You run out of Scotch tape before you run out of wrapping paper.

You run out of bows before you run out of wrapping paper.

You run out of wrapping paper before you run out of presents.

You know it's Christmas when . . .

Your pup has opened at least three packages under the tree, and chewed on at least three more, and it's not even December 15 yet.

You count how many times you hear someone say "reindeers" in a song.

You realize how much
you miss the people
you no longer have.

Your First Christmas Gift

It is Christmas Eve. The clock has struck ten p.m. The season's bustling and scurrying has ended. The house has come down with a calmness. Your windows shine with the dim light of candles. You and your family sit quietly in the dark corners of the room, staring at the only light on, the glistening and blinking lights of this year's Christmas tree. Another year has almost passed and the most anticipated day is about to come.

Everyone daydreams about the odd-shaped package or that strange rattle with the neatly wrapped paper. What could I be getting and will they like what I got them? Did I spend too much or not enough? Is it the right color or size? Does it match their personality? Will it be forgotten by New Year's, what took me three months to find? Will I get what I really want and will it top last year's?

Then the question is asked among the tree-gazers. "What do you want for Christmas?" After a circle of answers, the next question asks, "What has been your best present ever?" The first answer comes quickly from the young boy, "My bicycle I got last year!"

Trying to top her older brother, the girl proudly says it was her two-story doll house. The smiling mother said it had to be the engagement ring just ten years ago. After a little prying, the father gave the standard seasonal answer, "My best present is seeing all of you happy, healthy, and together."

Every year seems to top the next. But this year, remember the first and greatest gift to everyone. The gift came wrapped but needed no opening. It did not cost a cent. We never outgrow it like that bicycle. It does not break and take up space like the doll house. And it never loses its shine like that tarnished engagement ring. The gift is never out of style and always brings a peaceful, secure, and loving nature with it. And most of all, it is for all ages. Our first and greatest gift was Jesus. This Christmas, take a moment to tell God, thank you for giving us Your Son.

You know it's Christmas when . . .

You've watched the last five minutes of *It's a Wonderful Life* and heard Harry Bailey toast his brother and say, "To my big brother, George. The richest man in town."

You stand in line for twenty minutes at the grocery store with a frozen turkey in your hands while every woman in front of you writes a check . . . and takes her time (and yours) doing it. And you smile through it all because it's Christmas.

The Barn

It

was just

a humble shed

where the animals

went to sleep. A salvation

from the evil cold for the cattle

and the sheep. It housed the lowest

beast and even once a King. Its walls had

heard braying, and even angels sing. A floor,

crude and earthen, scattered with dry leaves. A roof,

worn and holey, of tied and thatched sheaves. Walls of

baked bricks, cured mud and sod, a most

unlikely birthplace for the only Son of God.

You know it's Christmas when . . .

You sit by just the lights of the tree
and listen to "Silent Night" and
count your blessings.

You have all the family in for dinner and someone
leaves their camera or present, and you have to
take it to them the next day.

You realize how happy the people
around you make you feel.

You know it's Christmas when . . .

You ride in the Christmas parade on a float and watch the little faces looking back at you as if you were magic.

You see someone you used to love while Christmas shopping.

You drink a glass of eggnog.

When Joseph Dreamed

Joseph dreamed of having a life,
One that would be simple and fair.
All he wanted was a faithful spouse,
To start a family that they could share.

Joseph dreamed of being a husband,
And promised each day he would live
To fulfill the comfort of a woman
And give to her the love only a husband can give.

Joseph dreamed of raising a child,
And teaching him the goodness of life.
He hoped his son would succeed in truth,
And never suffer the shames of strife.

Joseph dreamed of being a father,
His son's traits to him belong.
To preach to him the virtue of faith,
And the difference between right and wrong.

But then one night Joseph dreamed
Of an angel who brought him news,
Of how the Lord had gifted his wife
With a child who would pay our dues.

Joseph never dreamed of how it would be
To have God curry him favor.
And Joseph never dreamed to be the father
Of a long-awaited Savior.

Rudolph The Red-Nosed Reindeer

1. Who is the narrator?
2. What is the snowman's name?
3. Which reindeer is Rudolph's father?
4. What is the name of the town?
5. Hermie the Elf doesn't like to make toys. What does he want to be?
6. What is the name of Rudolph's girlfriend?
7. What is Bumbles the Abominable Snowmonster's one weakness?
8. Yukon Cornelius captures and reforms Bumbles, and then brings him back to Christmastown to the people. What "tall order" does Bumbles fulfill that finds favor with people?

Bonus: What instrument does Sam the snowman play?

Rudolph The Red-Nosed Reindeer Answers

1. Burl Ives
2. Sam
3. Donner (Donder)
4. Christmastown
5. A dentist
6. Clarise
7. Water—he can't swim
8. Because he was so tall, he put the star on top of the tree that no one could reach

Bonus: The banjo

Movie Quiz

1. Elizabeth Lane (Barbara Stanwyck) wrote articles for what magazine?
2. What kind of articles did she write?
    A. Homemaking
    B. Cooking
    C. Sewing
3. Who owned the magazine?
4. Who wrote all of Elizabeth's recipes for her?
5. Elizabeth mentioned in an article she was searching for a rocking chair and her readers sent her how many?
6. What hostess gift did Jefferson Jones (Dennis Morgan) bring Elizabeth when he arrived at the farm in Connecticut?
7. Jefferson was lost at sea for how many days?
8. What Christmas carol did Jefferson sing and play on the piano while Elizabeth decorated the tree?
9. To stop the wedding ceremony, what did Uncle Felix say the baby swallowed?
10. What did Elizabeth and Jefferson get arrested for doing?

Bonus: What was John Sloan's (Reginald Gardiner's) occupation?

Christmas in Connecticut

Movie Quiz Answers

1. *Smart Housekeeping*
2. B. Cooking
3. Alexander Yardley (Sidney Greenstreet)
4. Felix (S. Z. Sakall)
5. 38
6. A rocking chair
7. 18
8. "O Little Town of Bethlehem"
9. A gold watch
10. Stealing a horse and sleigh

Bonus: Architect

You know it's Christmas when . . .

You put a bow or a wreath on the grill of your car.

You eat a piece of coconut cake with custard.

You leave a few small, simple gifts
to buy on Christmas Eve.

It's All Good Today

I always like to leave something to buy on Christmas Eve. Whether it's stocking stuffers, a book for Mom, a tie for Dad, or even a gift certificate, I have to have one last reason to soak up the hustle and bustle of the season.

So one December 24th, I was walking down our quaint but busy downtown main street, ducking in stores as a quick haven from the blistery winter day. Decorations, lights, hot cider, lit candles, street lamp wreaths, and, of course, music inundated the entire scene. My shopping was basically finished, everyone in my family was home this year, and the weatherman was telling me there was a ninety percent chance of snow for early morning. The spirit of Christmas had intoxicated any worry or concern that I may have had and to say the least, life was good.

I exited the jewelry store with a reciprocating "Merry Christmas" to the clerk, and made my way to the corner. I stopped at the crosswalk and saw Clarks, an old man who frequents our downtown. Now some see Clarks as an offensive bum, others see him as an annoying eyesore, and most just ignore him. He earned his name because of his love for the Clark candy bar; just as George Burns always had a cigar, Clarks always had a Clark bar. For some reason (maybe my heart is a little softer) I find him harmless and a character who completes the typical small-town persona. And for some reason, whenever I see him, I spot him the loose change in my pocket. It started out as a random act of kindness on a good day, but has matured into an expectation from Clarks.

As I crossed the street, I noticed that Clarks had now noticed me and there was no chance of escaping another handout. Preparing for the encounter, I reached into my pocket to sort out a couple of ones from the higher bills. I suddenly paused in a panic realizing that I had only a fifty and two twenties. I really didn't want to raise the level of expectation and outdo myself by giving him twenty dollars. I thought, "He'll only waste it on candy or cigarettes or something stronger. Why should I endorse him for that?" But a wave of Christmas spirit billowed through me and I folded the crisp Jackson in my hand for the healthiest transaction yet.

Before I could approach him, I heard him yell out to me, "Hey Teacher! How you be?"

(He calls me Teacher because he thinks my glasses make me look smart.)

I took a few steps toward him and responded, “Great Clarks! And how are you doing?”

He quipped back, “Oh, I was better but I got over it.”

I decided that our relationship was nothing more beyond small talk, so I started to slip him the money and be on my way. I shook his hand with the money cupped inside and told him the usual, “You take care.”

Then to my surprise, he pulled his hand back and retreated a couple of steps while shaking his head and said, “No, no, Teacher, I’m good.”

Puzzled and possibly insulted I asked, “You’re good? What do you mean, Clarks?”

He then stared me in the eye and shared his truth.

“You know, Teacher, you always give me a few bucks when I ask you for it. But today, I’m good. I’m good today.”

Now he was nodding his head and began walking away

mumbling one more time, "I'm good today."

He left me standing on the sidewalk in a confused manner still wondering why he refused my charity.

Thankfully, I remembered that the Lord works in mysterious ways and Clarks was one of them. A phrase so simple as "I'm good today," can very quickly reveal one of the true sentiments of Christmas.

Clarks was obviously thankful that he made it through yesterday, and not a bit worried about tomorrow, but the fact is, is that it's all good today. Clarks reminded me of Paul's words in 2 Corinthians when he tells us, "Now is the time of God's favor, now is the day of salvation."

I walked straight to the convenience store, Clarks' hangout, and gave the cashier that twenty-dollar bill in my hand and told him it was for candy whenever Clarks comes in again. He smiled and assured me that Clarks would get his twenty bucks' worth and this secret was only between us. I walked out of the store and saw the old street-wanderer make his way to the next block. It was then I realized the irony in that he calls me Teacher, but I was the one who learned one of the most valuable lessons in my life. Thanks, Clarks.

You know it's Christmas when . . .

You cut and drag your own tree out of the woods.

You buy someone something special
you wish you had yourself.

You stand on the sidewalk with
a red nose and numb toes
and wave as Santa goes by.

Santa Claus is Coming to Town

1. Who is the narrator?
2. What was the majestic occupation or "difficult responsibility" of the ancestors of the Kringles?
3. What is the name of Kris Kringle's pet penguin?
4. Who is the ruler of the city of the people?
5. And what is the name of the city of the people?
6. Why are the people in this city so "somber"?
7. With what toy did the Burgermeister Meisterburger break his own law?
8. What happened when Kris Kringle gave Winter Warlock a toy choo-choo?
9. Kris Kringle tells Winter Warlock that changing his outlook on life is as easy as what?

Santa Claus is Coming to Town

10. What special toy did Kris Kringle deliver to Susan, a very sick girl in Sombertown?
11. Where did Kris Kringle hide the toys for the kids so the guards would not find them?
12. To avoid being caught by the guards of Sombertown, what two changes did Kris Kringle make?
13. What special event in Mr. Claus' life took place on Christmas Eve?
14. How did Mr. Claus earn the name of "Santa"?

BONUS: According to the movie, what was Mrs. Claus' first name?

Answers on next page

Santa Claus is Coming to Town Answers

1. Fred Astaire
2. The first toy makers to the King
3. Topper
4. Burgermeister Meisterburger
5. Sombertown
6. Burgermeister Meisterburger made it against the law to play with toys
7. A yo-yo
8. The Winter Warlock's icy heart was melted
9. Putting one foot in front of the other
10. A Noah's Ark
11. In their stockings
12. He took on the name of Claus and grew a beard
13. His marriage to Mrs. Claus
14. The townsfolk thought his deeds were very good and "saintly"

Bonus: Jessica

You know it's Christmas when . . .

You get out your Christmas ties.

You get out your Christmas sweaters.

Thanksgiving dinner is over.

The Drooping Halo

About three years ago, the best I remember
I was Christmas shopping in mid-December
And saw a little boy alone in the mall.

I approached him and could not stand the drama
When he told me that he had lost his mama
Then his face grew long and he began to bawl.

It turned out his mother was two stores down
And she thanked me profusely for her son had been found
Then hugged him tightly and gave him a little speech.

I left them to resume my holiday shopping
And then saw a man on crutches hopping
Trying for a toy he couldn't reach.

I quickly offered my height to help
For the toy he wanted was on the top shelf
And he beamed with joy from the assistance that I shared.

As I made my way through a crowded store
My conscience wouldn't let me walk by and ignore
The sight of an elderly woman in a wheelchair.

This lady wasn't there to buy, just to sell
Her propitious heart and to simply ring a bell
From hours on end to sit by a red metal pot.

I unpocketed some dollars, and gave three or four
Stuffed them in a can that was hungry for more
And justified my share from not earning a lot.

She smiled and said, "May God bless you."
I returned her gesture and blessed her, too
And tried once more to finish my shopping spree.

But it was later that night, sitting alone
And thinking of that woman with no legs of her own,
I was staring at the angel atop my tree.

I recalled the crippled man, and boy I found
And added up the deeds that would star my crown
And hoped the Lord would reward with such praise.

Then I thought of that woman, her bell's joyous rings
She needs no legs for she has wings
She's an angel keeping watch on us throughout our days.

And even though I served the Lord in a way
By helping some people and brightening their day
Should I be so humble to even think or say so?

You see, that angel's wheelchair
was merely a disguise
A pinch on the arm
to make me realize
The crown I'm wearing
is just a drooping halo.

You know it's Christmas when . . .

You see Santa
at the mall . . .

and ten minutes
later downtown.

You know it's Christmas when . . .

Someone throws out a gift
with all the used wrapping paper
on Christmas morning.

You and your best friend go
shopping together and eat lunch.

Your family draws names
and you get Aunt Edna's.

You know it's Christmas when . . .

You go to the firehouse lot and pick out a tree that you think is just the right size.

You get the tree home and discover the den has shrunk.

They turn the Christmas lights on downtown.

Christmas Music Quiz

1. Who wrote "White Christmas"?
2. In "The Chipmunk Song," what does Alvin want for Christmas?
3. What carol is Martin Luther credited with writing?
4. On the sixth day of Christmas, my true love gave what to me?
5. Which of these generally considered Christmas songs are not really Christmas songs?
    a. "Winter Wonderland"
    b. "Let It Snow"
    c. "Frosty, the Snowman"
    d. "Sleigh Ride"
    e. "Jingle Bells"
6. In "Away in a Manger," what does "the cattle are lowing" mean?
7. On the twelfth day of Christmas, my true love gave what to me?
8. In "Hark! The Herald Angels Sing," who are reconciled?
9. The line "born is the King of Israel" is from what carol?
10. In what movie did Bing Crosby first sing "White Christmas"?

Bonus: What carol is sung at the end of *It's a Wonderful Life*?

Answers

1. Irving Berlin
2. A hula hoop
3. “Away in a Manger”
4. Six geese a-laying
5. None are Christmas songs
6. Mooing
7. Twelve lords a-leapin’
8. God and sinners
9. “The First Noel”
10. *Holiday Inn*

Bonus: “Hark! The Herald Angels Sing”

The Christmas Story Quiz

Children's Level

1. Whose birthday is Christmas?
2. The baby Jesus was born in what city?
3. What was baby Jesus' mother's name?
4. What was His father's name?
5. When He was born, His mother took the baby Jesus and laid Him in what?
6. The first people to visit the baby came from the fields where they were tending their sheep. What were they called?
7. The next people to visit Him traveled a long distance and brought Him gifts. Who were these men?
8. How many gifts did they bring?
9. What were the gifts?
10. They found the baby Jesus by looking up and following something. What did they follow?

Bonus: On what date do we celebrate Christmas?

The Christmas Story Quiz

Children's Level Answers

1. Jesus
2. Bethlehem
3. Mary
4. Joseph
5. A manger
6. Shepherds
7. Wise Men
8. Three
9. Gold, Frankincense, and Myrrh
10. A star

Bonus: December 25th

Adult Level

1. Were Mary and Joseph married when Mary became pregnant?
2. What was Joseph's reaction?
3. What changed his mind?
4. Who named Jesus?
5. Why were Mary and Joseph traveling to Bethlehem?
6. How did they travel?
7. Were they married at this time?
8. What did the innkeeper actually say to Mary and Joseph?
9. What was the innkeeper's name?
10. In what sort of place was Jesus born?

Bonus: What animals were there?

Adult Level Answers

1. No
2. He wanted to break the engagement.
3. A visit from an angel
4. The angel
5. To be taxed in his ancestral city
6. No one knows
7. Not sure. "Espoused" was somewhere between an engagement and a marriage. Promised but not consummated
8. The innkeeper is not quoted.
9. No innkeeper is even mentioned.
10. There is no mention of a barn or a stable.

Bonus: No mention of any animals

Adult Level II

1. Who visited the baby that first night?
2. What is a manger?
3. How many Wise Men were there?
4. How did the Wise Men travel?
5. What is a Wise Man?
6. What did the star in the east do?
7. When the Wise Men arrived, where was the baby?
8. What is frankincense?
9. What is myrrh?
10. How many accounts of the Christmas story are in the Bible?

Bonus: Where are they found?

Adult Level II Answers

1. Shepherds only
2. An animal feeder
3. No one knows. We only know there were more than one.
4. No one knows.
5. A scholar, an astrologer
6. It led them to the baby and then stopped and stood over where he lay.
7. In a house
8. A gum resin from certain Asian trees used in perfume
9. A plant resin used in ancient embalming
10. Two

Bonus: Matthew and Luke

Minister's Level

1. Who was the father of Jesus?
2. How many times did an angel, through a dream, visit Joseph?
3. An angel told Joseph to call his son Jesus, which is the Greek form of Joshua, which means what?
4. Matthew 1:22 says, "Now all this was done, that it might be fulfilled which was spoken of the Lord by the prophet." To which prophet is this verse referring?
5. The wise men responded to King Herod with an earlier prediction by a prophet who said the messiah would be born in Bethlehem. Which prophet stated this?
6. Joseph took his wife and son to Egypt to avoid King Herod. Which Old Testament author prophesied: "Out of Egypt I have called my son"?
7. Name three other Biblical sons whose births were announced by an angel of the Lord.
8. Eight days after His birth, who was the "just and devout" man in the temple who blessed Jesus in accordance with the custom of the law?
9. Who was Jesus' grandfather?
10. How many generations were there from Abraham, the father of the faithful, through Jesus?

Bonus: What do the words "Messiah" and "Christ" mean?

Minister's Level Answers

1. The Holy Spirit (Matthew 1:20)
2. Four (Matthew 1:20, Matthew 2:13, Matthew 2:19, Matthew 2:22)
3. The Lord saves (Matthew 1:21)
4. Isaiah (Isaiah 7:14)
5. Micah (Micah 5:2)
6. Hosea (Hosea 11:1)
7. Isaac (Genesis 18:10), Samson (Judges 13:3), John the Baptist (Luke 1:13)
8. Simeon (Luke 2:34)
9. According to Matthew 1:16, Jacob
   According to Luke 3:23, Heli
10. 42 (Matthew 1:17)

Bonus: The Anointed One

You know it's Christmas when . . .

You taste a cup of oddly colored punch with a hint of some spice you can't readily identify.

Someone wears a Christmas tie to an office party that plays "Grandma Got Run Over By A Reindeer."

You say Merry Christmas to a total stranger.

You know it's Christmas when . . .

Your six-year-old tells you on Christmas Eve that he has changed his favorite football team from the Cowboys to the Redskins.

Ms. Griffen's Christmas Candle

When someone asks me about my favorite Christmas memory, I usually warm up by telling them about my brother and me helping Paw Paw carry in presents from the trunk of his car to the trunk of the tree. While I'm replaying these detailed memories of every Christmas Eve, I remind myself of those holiday smells seeping from the kitchen, where my mom was cooking six different things, and yet still humming the harmony line to the Ray Conniff Singers on the radio. And although I start to laugh a little remembering how Davey and I would fight over who would get to carry the bigger presents in the house, so we could peek at the tags, for some reason now, I tend to cry a little thinking about that.

Then there was the Christmas morning when we came downstairs to find a floor full of presents with a nine-foot pine tree lying on top of them all. Broken glass balls, twisted tinsel, and an angel with a crooked halo adorned the entire—and I mean the entire—living room. I was crying, Davey was quiet, Mom was giggling because of her two hours of sleep, and Dad—well, he was a bit irritated due to his two hours of sleep. But he was quick to recover when he got down on his knee, put his arms around me and Davey and said, "Boys, you know Santa Claus had a lot of houses to get to last night, and I believe he was a little behind and in a hurry, and when he slung that big sack across his back to go up the chimney, all of those toys must have knocked the tree down!" We quickly forgave Santa for destroying our tree and Dad had just given us more proof that Santa was in the house the night before.

Oh, and of course, I can't leave out my sixteenth Christmas when Amy, a perfect little short-haired sophomore, and I had only been seeing each other "seriously" for three weeks before Christmas. I didn't think we'd been in a relationship long enough to get each other something for Christmas, but Mom (who thought Amy was so cute) thought otherwise. So Christmas Eve, Davey and I were standing in the jewelry store when we narrowed it down to a gold necklace or a picture frame. That night when I picked her up, she confessed she didn't buy me anything. She said she just wanted to ride around, look at the lights, listen to Christmas music, and just be with me. Wow! What a gift. Every time I see colored lights and wreaths on windows, or hear "The Christmas Song" on the radio, I swear I can smell her perfume on the collar of my shirt. And by the way, I gave her the necklace and the picture frame.

But as much as these memories lie heavy on my heart, there is still one that affects me a little more. I can remember looking out the window and down the snow-covered street, and seeing old Ms. Griffen sitting in her chair reading a book by candlelight. It was Christmas Eve; I was nine years old and bursting with the holiday spirit, when Mom called me into the kitchen. She had a plate of leftover stuffing balls and sugar cookies that she wanted me to take to Ms. Griffen. I shrugged around and tried to finagle my way out of the saintly deed of a simple delivery with a number of weak excuses. Finally, Mom wiped her hands on her apron and sternly commanded, "You are taking this food to Ms. Griffen and that's that." I had no choice. I grabbed my coat and gloves, marched out the door, and headed down the street.

Now Ms. Griffen was not considered an invalid; it's just that the neighborhood never saw her go out of her house much. There was always something kind of spooky or weird about her, because she never talked, or waved, or even turned lights on inside her house. I must admit I was a bit scared when I found myself standing on her porch, and I hesitated right before I was about to knock on the door. I knocked the usual three times and the door gently creaked half open. I could make out a dim outline of a frail lady with a cane almost as feeble as she was.

Before I could say whatever it was I was going to say, she very confidently offered, "Merry Christmas. Won't you please come in?" Instead of answering her, and instead of dropping the plate and running, I stepped onto that fading brown carpet and was surrounded with the immediate warmth of an old wood stove. She then offered me a glass of eggnog, and even though I never did like it much, I accepted. She told me what a thoughtful person my mother was as she sat the plate of leftovers on the coffee table. She disappeared into her dark kitchen and left me in the room alone. I looked around and my only company was a plate of food, a smudged pair of reading glasses and a Bible. It seemed like forever, but when she returned with my eggnog, she told me, "Sit for a minute. I want to read you something." Before I realized it, I was sitting in front of her, surprisingly anxious to hear what she was going to say. She picked up her glasses and the tattered book on the table, opened it, and began reading.

And an angel of the Lord appeared to them, and the glory of the Lord shone around them, and they were filled with fear. And the angel said to them, "Be not afraid; for behold, I bring you good news of a great joy which will come to all the people; for to you is born this day in the city of David, a Savior, who is Christ the Lord."

She closed the book and sat quietly in thought. All I could see was the silhouette of a tender old woman contoured by the shimmering glow of the candle in the window behind her. Suddenly, I felt a comforting peace that swelled throughout my nine-year-old body. I drank the last sip of my eggnog and stood up. I then walked over to her, kissed her on the cheek, and told her, "Merry Christmas." She then gingerly whispered to me, "Thank you my child, for making my Christmas merry." I turned to walk out the door and gave one last glance to my new friend. As I struggled to find the words of "thank you," I saw a tear stream down her cheek and rest safely in the corner of a smile. I closed the door, walked home, hugged Mom and Dad, and went upstairs to get ready for bed. After saying my prayers and before falling asleep, I peeped under the window shade and stared down the dark quiet street, and saw only the flickering of Ms. Griffen's lonely candle. I closed my eyes, said one more prayer, and fell fast asleep.

Every Christmas Eve, I go to church for the candlelight service. The minister reads the ageless story of the birth of Jesus. The children sing "Silent Night." Poinsettias saturate the altar in memory of loved ones. Then we all stand to sing "Joy to the World" and the lights of the sanctuary begin to dim. The elders pass out candles and we all wait in silence while the minister lights his candle. He then recites the familiar old words of an angel of the Lord:

> *I bring you good news of a great joy, which will come to all the people; for to you is born this day in the city of David, a Savior, who is Christ the Lord.*

I then light my candle and gaze at the flame dancing on the wick. As I watch the wax carefully drip from the candle, I see that tear streaming down Ms. Griffen's face. And then I remember her smile, and I begin to cry. I whisper to myself those same words she whispered to me: "Thank you Ms. Griffen, for making *all* my Christmases merry."

You know it's Christmas when . . .

A little round-faced boy in the
Nativity play, dressed as a shepherd,
smiles real big and waves at his mother.

Every candle in the house has melted
into a messy mound of beautiful memories.

Daddy says grace.

There is No Quiet in Bethlehem

Babies are born in pink and blue
And wrapped in satins and laces.
They smell of milk and powdered perfume
And have round and cherubic faces.
They're cradled and cooed and nursed and fed
And rocked so gently to sleep
By mothers who pray at the end of each day
The Lord their souls to keep.

There is no quiet in Bethlehem
The streets are jammed and loud,
Turmoil, confusion and near-panic
From the overflowing crowd.
Private homes and public inns
Are turning travelers away.
Old and young sleep in the streets,
There's no place else to stay.

Old men who can barely walk
Babies who have not yet learned how,
Young men, bone-weary and tired,
Drop and rest wherever the laws allow.
Even very young women, pregnant with child
And nearing the ends of their terms,
Cannot find a simple, clean room,
Private and free of germs.

What if a baby were born tonight
In this dusty, crowded city?
Would anyone hear the labor cries?
Would they care or even have pity?
Could a human baby actually be born
Like a cow or a pig on the ground,
If a mother-to-be should suddenly be
A mother tonight in this town?

The dirt and the stench of a stable floor
Might be the first air in his chest,
And a feeder box used by sheep
Might be his first bed of rest.
The stink and unsanitary surroundings
Would be filthy and shameful at least.
But a baby would never be born in a barn.
That's only fit for a beast.

No, babies are born in pink and blue
And wrapped in satins and laces.
They smell of milk and powdered perfume
And have round and cherubic faces.
No baby of yours or mine would dare
Be caught born among such things:
For to be born in a barn, in a stall, in the hay
Is fit only for beasts and Kings.

You know it's Christmas when . . .

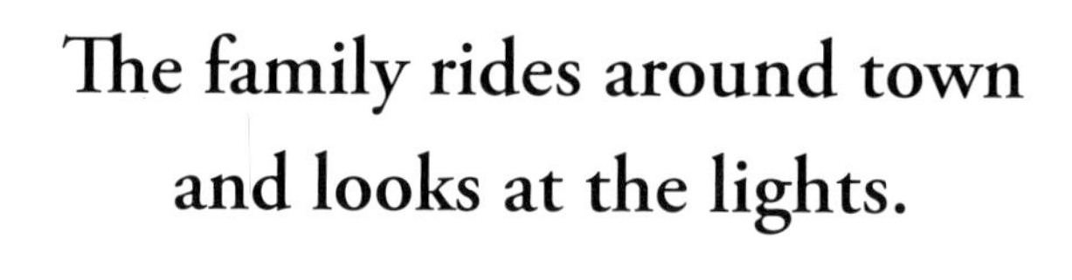

The family rides around town
and looks at the lights.

You buy gifts for someone
less fortunate than yourself.

You leave cookies and milk for Santa
and a bucket of water for Rudolph.

You know it's Christmas when . . .

Everyone goes to grandma's house and one of the grandkids breaks something and she says, "Don't worry about it. It was old." No matter how valuable it was.

You drop a coin in the kettle.

You put a wreath on someone's grave and stand for a minute and have Christmas with them.

White Christmas Movie Quiz

1. What did Captain Davis (Danny Kaye) do for Captain Wallace (Bing Crosby) that earned him a partnership in the musical act?
2. Who played the Haynes sisters?
3. What state are the Haynes sisters headed to for Christmas?
4. Who is the owner of the country inn in this state?
5. Why is business so slow at the inn?
6. When Bing can't sleep, what does he count instead of sheep?
7. What do Vera-Ellen and Danny Kaye do in order to push Rosemary Clooney and Bing Crosby closer together?
8. How does Bob Wallace (Crosby) get the Christmas Eve invitation out to all the men in General Waverly's infantry?

Bonus: What is the name of the inn?

White Christmas Movie Quiz Answers

1. Captain Davis saved Captain Wallace's life from a falling brick wall in the war.
2. Rosemary Clooney and Vera-Ellen
3. Vermont
4. General Waverly, the former general of Wallace and Davis during the war
5. There is no snow.
6. His blessings
7. They get engaged.
8. He makes the announcement on the famous Ed Harrison TV Show.

Bonus: The Columbia Inn

You go to a candlelight service
at church and drip wax on:

Your new dress

Your new suit

Your new shoes

Someone else's new shoes

The pew

The carpet

The hardwood floor

(Ouch!) Your fingers

You know it's Christmas when . . .

You discover you're two batteries short.

You try to wrap a basketball.

There are more pine needles on
the floor than on the tree.

Christmas Vacation Movie Quiz

1. What did the Griswolds forget once they found their tree in the wilderness?
2. What does Clark Griswold (Chevy Chase) want to buy with his bonus check?
3. What are the names of the Griswolds' neighbors?
4. How many lights does Clark put on the house?
5. What is Clark's aunt's name?
6. What does Clark's aunt wrap up as a present?
7. Who burns down the Griswold tree?
8. What is said as the dinner's grace (blessing)?
9. What part of the turkey does cousin Eddie (Randy Quaid) want?
10. What does Clark get as his bonus?
11. What does Eddie get Clark for Christmas?
12. Where does Clark get his second Christmas tree?
13. What jumped out of the second Christmas tree?

Bonus: What were the Griswolds' punch glasses shaped as?

Christmas Vacation Movie Quiz Answers

1. A saw
2. A swimming pool
3. Todd and Margo
4. 25,000 lights
5. Bethany
6. Her cat
7. Uncle Lewis by lighting his cigar
8. The Pledge of Allegiance
9. The neck
10. A one-year membership in the Jelly-of-the-Month Club
11. Clark's boss, Frank Shirley (Brian Doyle-Murray) with a bow
12. His own front yard
13. A squirrel

Bonus: Moose heads

You know it's Christmas when . . .

You come out of a store with an armful of packages and see snowflakes.

Your house smells like cookie dough, cedar, and scented candles.

You know it's Christmas when . . .

Your little girl plays "Away in a Manger" on the piano with both hands and you cry.

A Christmas Story Movie Quiz

1. Let's help the old man out on his newspaper trivia: What is the Lone Ranger's nephew's horse's name?
2. What does Ralphie want for Christmas?
3. What grade does Ralphie get on his What I Want For Christmas essay?
4. According to Ralphie, some folks are Baptists, some are Catholics. But what was his old man?
5. Who eats the Christmas turkey?
6. Where does the family wind up having Christmas dinner?
7. The narrator is very descriptive in describing the two bullies. What color are Scott Fargus' eyes?
8. Before the infamous leg lamp shows up, what does the old man think the prize might be?
9. Ralphie uses his Little Orphan Annie decoder to reveal what secret message?
10. When the "fragile" sweepstakes box shows up at the house, what language does the old man think is written on the crate?

Bonus: In what state does the story take place?

A Christmas Story Movie Quiz Answers

1. Victor
2. Red Ryder BB gun
3. C+
4. An Oldsmobile man
5. The neighbors' (Bumpass') dogs
6. At a Chinese restaurant
7. Yellow
8. A bowling alley
9. Be sure to drink your Ovaltine
10. Italian

Bonus: Indiana

You know it's Christmas when . . .

Someone wraps something real small in a real big box.

You hide a gift from someone and forget where you hid it.

At least four situation comedies parody Charles Dickens' *A Christmas Carol.*

You know it's Christmas when . . .

Your six-year-old yells for his mother at midnight on Christmas Eve from his bedroom and tells her he just heard the reindeer on the roof . . .

when what he really heard
was his Daddy falling down
the steps with a bicycle in his hands.

The Calm After The Storm

Do you ever wonder what it was like on March 11, 1876? This was the day after Alexander Graham Bell uttered the first words on a telephone. What about April 24, 1896? This was the day after the first successful public exhibition in the United States of motion pictures. Here's another one: December 18, 1903. The day after the Wright brothers celebrated the first flight of a machine that brought man closer to being a bird. If you were there on these days mentioned, would you have realized what a technological breakthrough you were witnessing? Could you have predicted the success and luxuries of these unimaginable feats? One thing is for sure: I can't imagine a world without them. But another thing is also for sure: air travel is more frustrating than convenient at times, movies are sending disappointing messages, and phone bills require a separate loan just to pay them. These "advances" obviously opened the door to a high-tech world and have brought a whirlwind of problems with them. We need more space, more money, higher prices, greater tolerance, less employment, reduced motivation, lots of stress and the list goes on. A storm is upon us.

But have you ever wondered what it was like the day before Jesus was born? I have. Once. And I didn't like it much. I wasn't sure if I knew what forgiveness was. I didn't know the sincerity of a sacrifice. I didn't know what "unconditional love" meant. I had no shadow behind me for encouragement or footsteps in front to guide me. And a prayer just wasn't complete without ending it "in Christ's name."

I realized rather quickly that I was somewhat hopeless, therefore helpless. I was lonely. And I was lost. It didn't take me long to know that I like Jesus in my world, and more appropriately, I'm glad he let me be in His. I want Jesus around anytime and everywhere in all the breaths of my life, and more so, I need Him around every time and anywhere in my life.

Jesus was a lot like a storm. He did not rain down strife and discord, but rather His reign made waves of inspiration and faith. His words have covered miles of sacred land and his love has flooded generations of followers. I am thankful and blessed that my head has been dipped into His pool of saving grace. This storm is very different and entirely unique compared to others. The time of peace and calm is not before this Storm, but after it, and what a wonderful time it is.

You know it's Christmas when . . .

You get a card from
someone you
weren't expecting
to hear from.

You know it's Christmas when . . .

That bowl of nuts
shows up on the
table by the sofa
with the nutcracker
and those sharp
little picks in it.

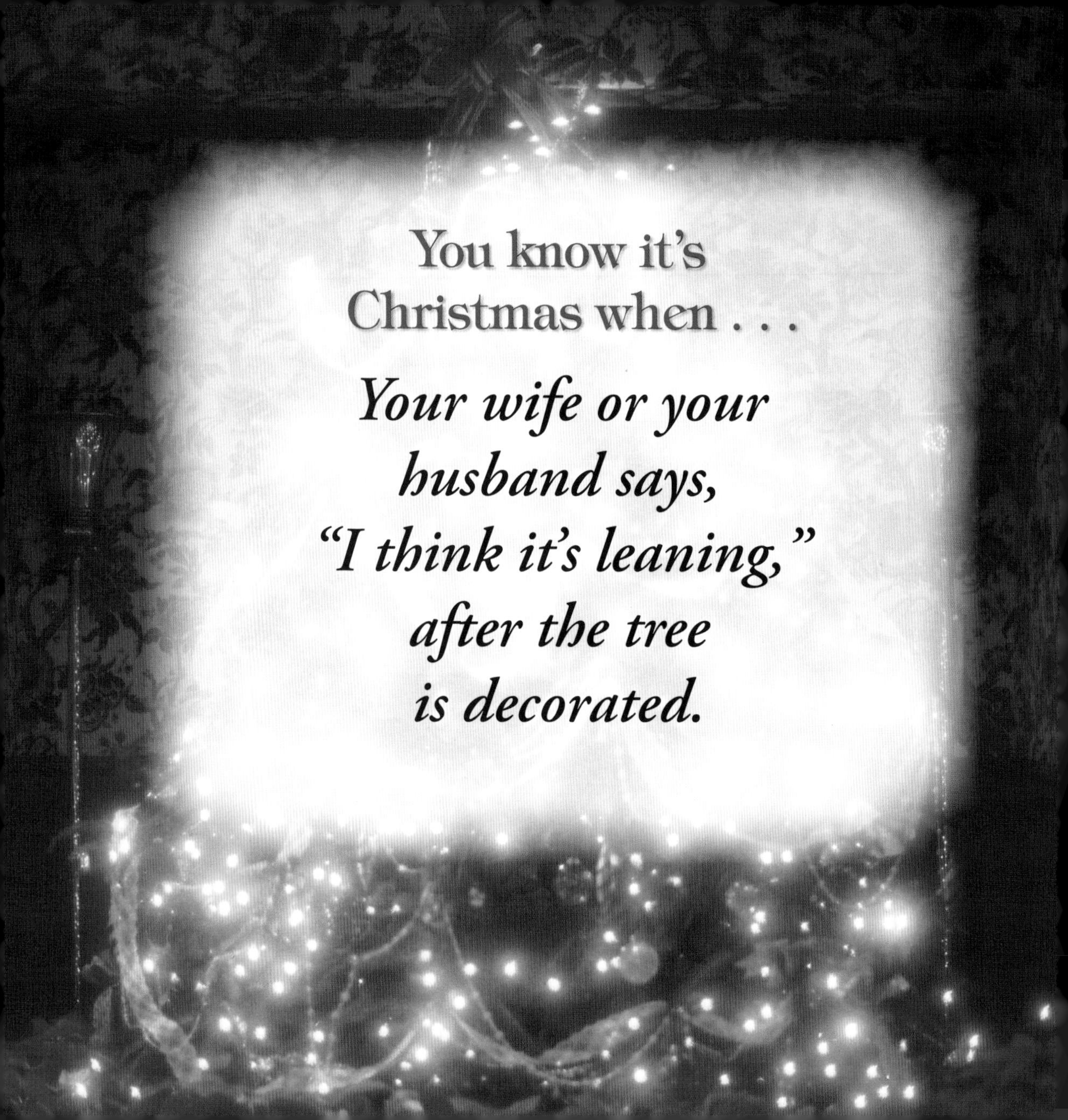
You know it's
Christmas when . . .
*Your wife or your
husband says,
"I think it's leaning,"
after the tree
is decorated.*

You know it's Christmas when . . .

You go Christmas caroling.

You go Christmas caroling at a nursing home, a hospital, a shut-in's house.

A group comes Christmas caroling in your front yard.

You know it's Christmas when . . .

Someone says, "You've got to come outside for your last gift." And you know it's a sled or a bike or a car or something really big.

You know it's Christmas when . . .

You stand in the department store line to get a gift wrapped longer than you stood in line to pay for it.

The Christmas Parade

I went to the Christmas parade last night
Saw Santa Claus and colored lights
Saw Christian floats and majorettes
Antique cars and bayonets
Carried by soldiers in perfect step
And dancing clowns, full of pep
Boy! Do I love parades!

I waved at the Snow Queen and she waved at me
I clapped for the Boy Scouts–Troop 33
I oohed and aahed at every sight
And hummed when the choir sang "Silent Night"
I touched my heart, then touched my eye
And saluted the flag as it passed by
Boy! Do I love parades!

But my favorite parts, I have to say
Are the marching bands and the songs they play
And no matter how far out of step and tune
They take me back, the drum and bassoon
To a time forty years ago tonight
When I marched and played "O Holy Night"
Boy! Do I still love parades!

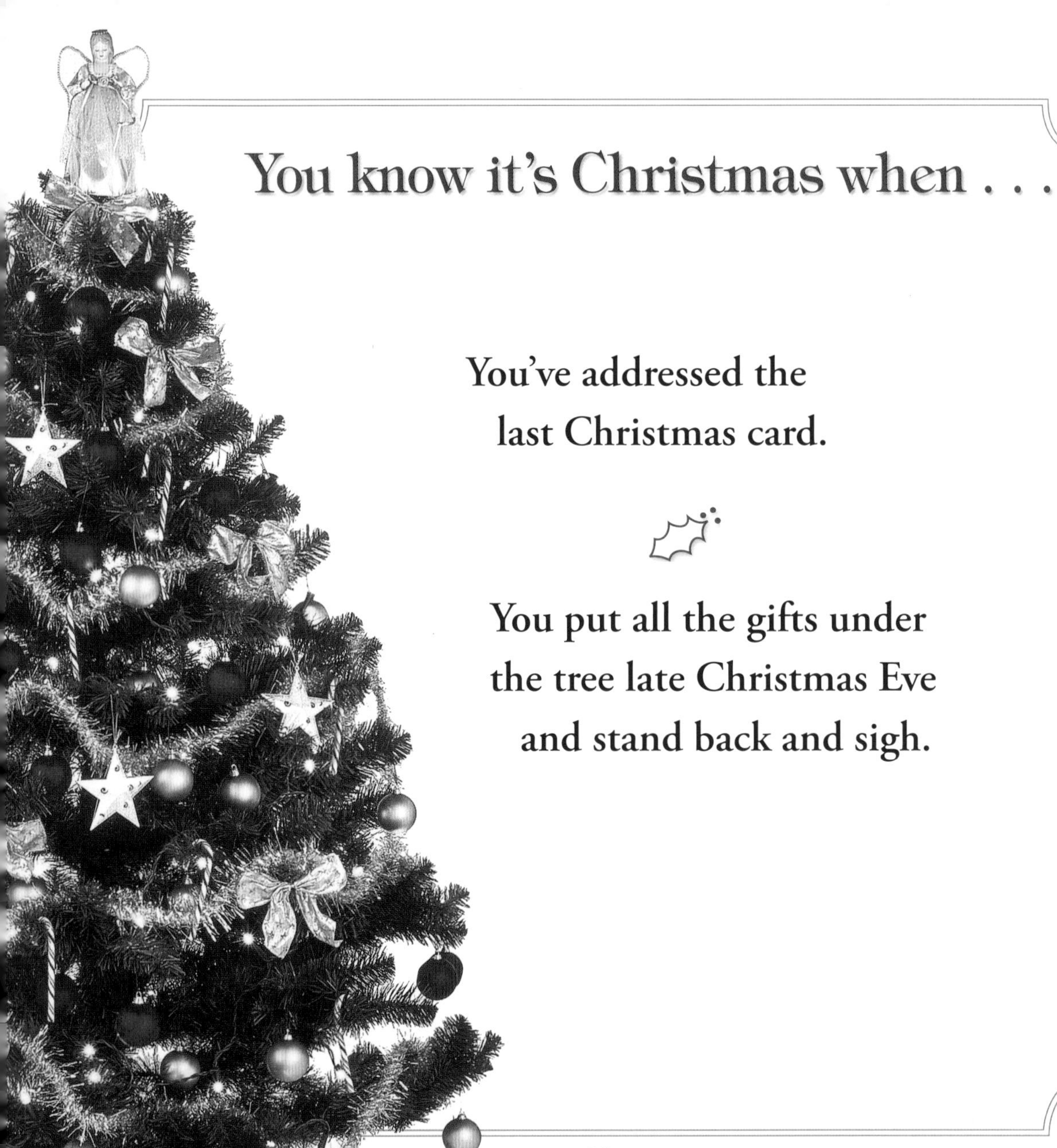

You know it's Christmas when . . .

You've addressed the
last Christmas card.

You put all the gifts under
the tree late Christmas Eve
and stand back and sigh.

You know it's Christmas when . . .

You say a prayer, just before bed on Christmas Eve, for the things you are really thankful for and no one will ever know what they are except you.

You know it's Christmas when . . .

Gene Autry sings "Rudolph The Red-Nosed Reindeer."

Bing Crosby sings "White Christmas."

You know it's Christmas when . . .
You've read the
story again
in Matthew
and Luke.

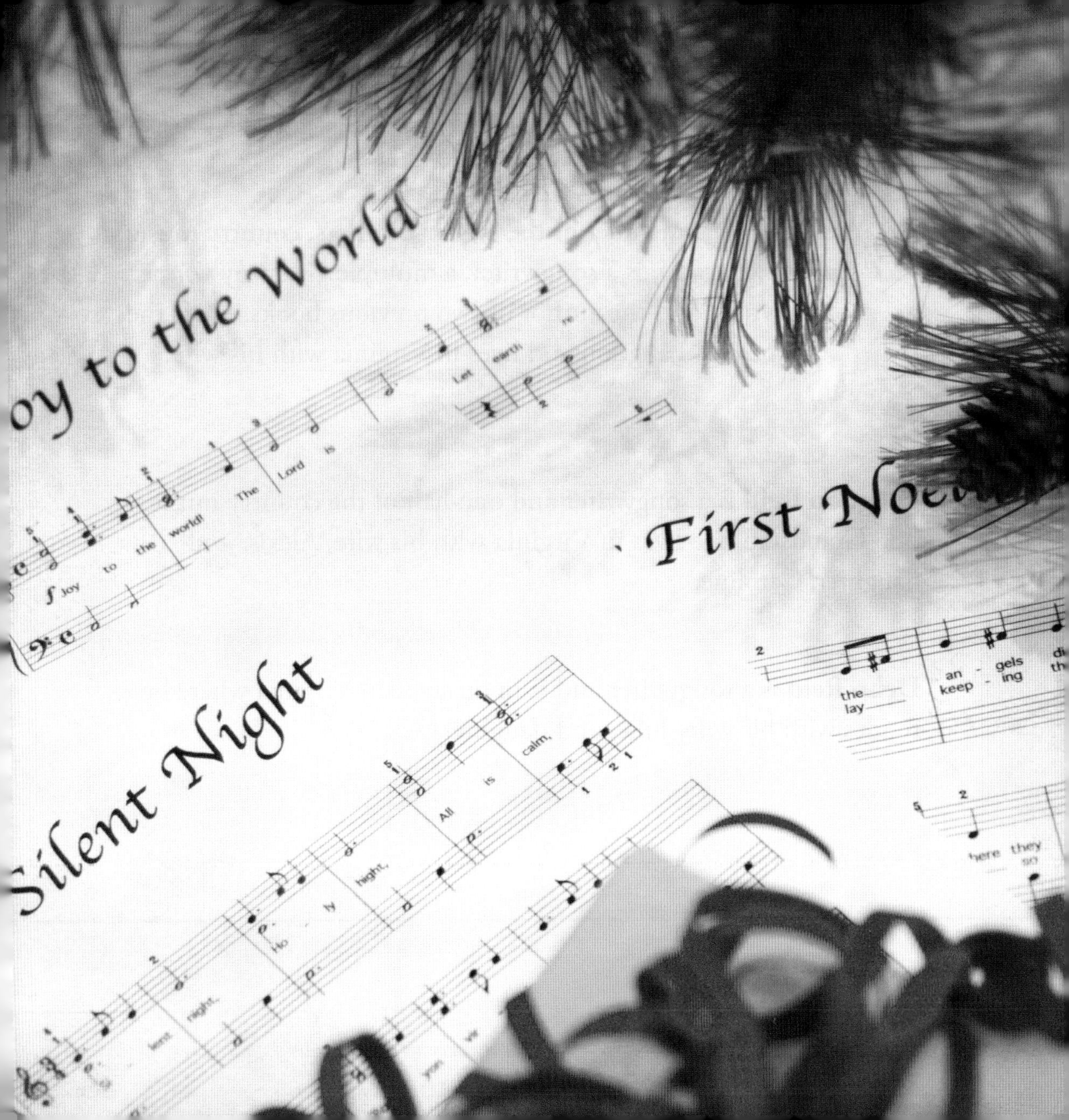

Joy to the World
Joy to the world! The Lord is
Let earth re-
First Noel
the angels did
lay keeping the
here they
Silent Night
Silent night, Holy night, All is calm,